JOHN C. DAVIS

Dark Psychology (2in1)

Emotional Manipulation & The Art of Reading People - Break The Cycle of Hidden Narcissistic Abuse, Set Boundaries & Reclaim Power Over Your Own Emotions

Contents

II   How To Analyze People: The Revealing
Power Of Facial Expressions

I

Dark Psychology Secrets: The Defense Guide Against Emotional Manipulation

Outsmart, Disarm and Survive The Toxic Emotional Abuser in Your Life & Reclaim Power Over Your Own Emotions

Read This First!

* * *

As a way of saying thank you for your purchase, I'd like to give you a **Free** gift!

The Cruelest Face of "Love" Revealed' is your essential quick-start guide to help you detect & escape high-conflict personalities in your life.

»CLICK HERE to download your FREE Guide now!«

*** *The offer expires in 24 hours so go ahead click the link and grab your copy now!*

Discover how manipulative people use **fear**, **obligation**, and **guilt** to push your buttons and leave you completely numb!

Understand how they hook you so insidiously and deceptively, so you can stop feeling guilty about missing red flags.

» Click Here to Get Your 100% Free Bonus Now!«

Introduction

From Pain To Power

Ultimately, each and every one of us is in pursuit of an enhanced emotional state, and what makes us happy varies greatly from person to person. That said, we all share an innate fear of being hurt by those around us, whether it's by a friend or a family member. Often, the most painful of these experiences originate from our most intimate relationships.

The chances are that, at some point, you will have fallen foul of a manipulator in your day to day life. They probably hurt you, and it is likely that you are aware of a few manipulative people with whom you have met or see on a regular basis, whether you are their victim or not.

What's more, numerous texts claim to demonstrate how you can use coercive techniques to better manipulate others. Therefore, it stands to reason that many of those around you may be bending you to their will in one way or another, whether you are aware of it or not.

The unavoidable, inevitable truth is that you are being manipulated. Whether you are aware of it or not. Whether the perpetrator is aware of it or not. Whether the manipulator is an individual or a vast, multinational entity. This is an undeniable fact, like it or not.

But there are precautions you can take, measures that you can put into place, and skills that you can learn that will, to some extent, protect you from manipulators. They are typically competitive people and, by educating yourself on the matter, you gain a competitive edge. With enough understanding of their methods, you can disarm a manipulator.

Whilst some people are blatant and harmful in their manipulations, and some are even proud to call themselves 'influencers', for many of us, morals and personal ethics get in the way of using such techniques of social manipulation for personal gain. The purpose of this book, therefore, is to inform you of the methods that they may use, not so that you can learn to manipulate others, but so that you can identify those who would use dark psychological techniques against you.

Consider the following a guide to psychological self-defense.

The Solution

How can we deal with manipulative individuals? The answer is multifaceted:

Firstly, we will familiarize ourselves with the types of manipulation and manipulative individuals that are most commonly encountered. For example, people with narcissistic personality types have been found to engage in social manipulation more than others.

Secondly, we make ourselves aware of the tell-tale signs of manipulation and manipulators.

By identifying the behaviors and mannerisms that are most commonly associated with social string-pulling, we can pick a manipulator out of a crowd, giving us the upper hand and the competitive edge so that we may deal with the perpetrator as we see fit.

Thirdly, we discuss methods that may be used to deal with such social encounters in a practical, hands-on manner. With an arsenal of pre-prepared sentences and statements at your disposal, and the tips contained in this book to utilize, you will find yourself feeling far better equipped to deal with the next manipulator that crosses your path.

The Benefits

There are many benefits to becoming more aware of how people might manipulate you, some obvious, and some less so.

There are always a few nasty surprises in life, but you will have a greater potential than others to avoid encounters with those that intend to exploit you. By being aware of how they operate, we can minimize our emotional distress.

Peace of mind and a lessened state of anxiety can be achieved, once you become confident in your ability to identify those harmful individuals around you. This understanding allows you to distance yourself from negative individuals, further minimizing the likelihood of being hurt.

All humans communicate non-verbally in various ways. By learning to analyze these signals, you can develop skills that may prove particularly helpful in your professional life as well as your social one. We can learn to monitor, anticipate and prepare for certain social situations.

You may also notice improvements in other non-harmful relationships. The reason for this is that, by teaching ourselves to study people, to analyze them to an extent, we become more aware of their needs, and can adjust our behavior accordingly. Furthermore, you may even find yourself more attuned to your own emotions after analyzing yourself. Consider this point as a bonus.

By opening up to an individual, we render ourselves vulnerable, not to say that anyone should avoid close relationships. However, this becomes especially apparent when we examine intimate and romantic relationships. By becoming more aware of our closest relationships, we see how one may be victimized in these most painful of social situations.

Where's the Proof?

All around you!

Manipulative psychological methods have been employed by entities on every level of society, from your next-door neighbor to your government. Corporations want you to buy their product. Cults and religions want you to pledge your allegiance. Terrorists want you to fear them and your partner wants you to wash the dishes.

All of these groups and individuals may be willing to use invasive psychological techniques to further their own agenda, no matter the scale of it.

Clearly, we don't need to look far for evidence that we are all made to dance like puppets from time to time.

What can I Hope to Learn?

After exploring some of the concepts in this book, you will find yourself gaining some, if not all, of the following skills:

- Improved ability to analyze other people's behaviors and to interpret their emotions.

- Greater confidence in your social interactions, knowing that you are in control.
- The ability to clearly distinguish between truth and lies.
- A greater understanding of your own vulnerabilities, and how to defend yourself despite them.
- Greater ease in working with a variety of individuals.
- Greater resistance to fallibility in your interactions.
- Greater awareness of methods that may be used by individuals, as well as by faceless, multinational entities.
- A greater sense of individuality, as you find yourself breaking away from the pack, thinking and acting on your own terms for a more gratifying existence.

What's the Rush?

Life is finite. The question is:

How long do you want to wait?

The sooner you come to understand the sinister nature of certain forces, the sooner you can break free from their manipulative, constraining hold and start living your own life.

It is important to remember that one cannot simply avoid pain forever. Social manipulation is a fact of life, but the information contained within this book, when interpreted and followed responsibly, can serve to minimize those moments of emotional agony.

Understanding Manipulation

"The basic tool for the manipulation of reality is the manipulation of words. If you can control the meaning of words, you can control the people who must use the words."
- Philip K. Dick

This chapter will touch on some popular theories of manipulative psychology and their origins, as well as which vulnerabilities are most commonly exploited by manipulators, and the motivations of such manipulators.

Beware of The Malevolent Dark Triad

The Dark Triad is a psychological theory that comprises a trilogy of personality traits. These are narcissism, Machiavellianism, and psychopathy. The Dark Triad, a term originally coined in the 1990s, has since received much support from numerous statistical studies of personality types.

Of these three personality traits, narcissism and Machiavellianism are most closely associated with manipulative social interactions, and the degree to which a person is Machiavellian can be measured on the "Mach scale." Numerous scales of narcissism exist.

Typically, individuals who score highly on the Mach scale

are, compared to most, lacking in concern for morality, unemotional in their interactions, and far more inclined to engage in social manipulation.

As there is an overlap between the three qualities of the Dark Triad, it pays to be aware that an individual who is particularly involved in one may also score highly in another. For example, a person who appears to be more narcissistic (vain, self-centered and egotistical) may also be especially psychopathic (lacking in empathy) or Machiavellian (prone to coercion and manipulation).

The Narcissist

Narcissism, whilst only one of a few personality traits associated with manipulative behavior, is a term understood by most of us, and is characterized by the following qualities:

- Vanity
- Egotism
- A sense of entitlement
- A need for admiration
- Self-centredness

Interestingly, popular psychoanalysis theories suggest that narcissism stems from an issue in which, as a baby, the individual was unable to distinguish themselves from other objects in the world around them. This difficulty gave birth to a feeling of insignificance, a need to tower over others, make their mark and be the very greatest member of their flock.

The most extreme narcissists can be said to have Narcissistic Personality Disorder, typically when their self-centered grandiosity grows to such an extent that it interferes with their daily lives and functions.

It has been estimated that around 1% of the population have Narcissistic Personality Disorder, but, as is the case with all personality traits, they exist on a scale, and most of us have narcissistic tendencies to some degree.

The Victim's Vulnerabilities

Some people are naturally more resistant to manipulative techniques, whilst others appear to attract manipulators. By becoming aware of the qualities that manipulators are looking for, we can minimize the likelihood that we are targeted. There are certain qualities that may render you more vulnerable to manipulation. These include:

- You have low self-esteem. Your defenses are low, and your lack of self-regard makes this especially obvious to manipulators.

- You are honest. Honesty is a great quality to have, but beware with whom you share your truths. Manipulators can more easily exploit someone they are certain will always tell the truth.

- You are very trusting. Trust should be earned. This may seem obvious, but it's surprising just how many of us are willing to put our trust in a complete stranger.

- You are highly empathetic. You want to help others and are willing to put yourself in a vulnerable position to do so.

- You struggle to maintain social boundaries. Manipulators are drawn to easy targets, and those with lower defense and ambiguous social boundaries are definitely the easiest.

In addition to the above points, people who crave attention, are naïve, lonely or immature may also find themselves to be targeted by manipulators. It's vital that we do what we can to maximize our resilience in these respects. By allowing yourself to be an easy target and broadcasting your vulnerability, you are practically inviting manipulators to exploit you.

Motivations of Manipulators

A manipulator may have one or several motivations. Some examples of these include:

A strong desire to be in control. They need to feel that they are pulling the strings, and not someone else.

The need to advance their own personal agenda and they may be willing to do this at any cost. This may be potentially criminal, or for financial or social gain.

The need for a sense of superiority. The feelings of power that a manipulator gets by manipulating brings him/her pleasure. This may even be a way of increasing their own self-esteem. It's quite possible that, by putting others down, they lift themselves up. Be cautious of those individuals who appear willing to back-stab and trample to get a rung or two up the social ladder.

A cure for boredom. This is certainly one of the darkest possible motivations for manipulation. The manipulator derives pleasure from making you do their bidding.

Unconscious manipulations. More innocently, a manipulator may not even be aware of his/her actions. It may be the case that the manipulator does not identify with the emotions of others. An example of a non-deliberate manipulation would be if your partner suffered from commitment phobia and a fear of becoming too attached to you, and this, therefore, enables them to rationalize their covert behaviors.

3 Toxic Sub-Types of Narcissism

Here are three archetypical, manipulative, narcissistic characters that you may even get the impression you have already met:

1. **The Charismatic Leader.** He swaggers around the office flexing his biceps and engaging in 'banter' whilst oozing false charm all over anyone who will listen. He is always the loudest voice in the room and certainly considers himself the most interesting. He is a textbook narcissist, pining for the attention and approval of everyone around him.

2. **The Oppressive Partner**. Your partner is overly protective and is prone to jealousy. They seem willing to go out of their way to keep you close all the time, and may even be pleased when certain things don't work out for you. They

hold you close, but it's out of fear as much as love.

3. **The Quiet One.** They brood in the corner at the office party, perhaps anxious, but absolutely judgemental. They look down their nose at everyone around them with an air of superiority. They might not say it aloud, but they think they are better than you and you can tell.

Think about whether these people seem <u>familiar</u> to you. It may pay to be cautious of anyone who fits these descriptions.

Take away points

1. Manipulators come in many forms, influencing others in many different ways.
2. Most manipulators will target those they perceive to be psychologically vulnerable.
3. Their motivations are varied, and not always as malicious as it may seem.
4. The field of psychology offers a wealth of academic literature on manipulation.

How To Identify a Manipulator

"Your greatest enemy will hide in the last place you would ever look"
– Caesar

Common Traits

There are a number of traits that the majority of manipulators share. By identifying these patterns and similarities, we can better prepare ourselves for real-life encounters with harmful social manipulators.

    1) **They know how to detect your weaknesses**. They can identify your vulnerabilities, which is why it is essential that you can identify them as well.

    2) **They will use these weaknesses against you**. Your vulnerabilities are like a back door to your mind, and most of the vicious manipulators you will encounter have absolutely no hesitations about letting themselves in.

    3) The manipulator will, once inside, help themselves to **whatever serves their self-centered needs.** This need may come in any form and may be different for every manipulator.

    4) And, once they have benefited, the **manipulator is likely to repeat-offend**. Once you have been taken advantage of, the

perpetrator will likely continue to do so, until you put a stop to the violations.

It helps to have an understanding of the traits that are commonly associated with 'narcissistic personality disorder' which, as mentioned above, correlates significantly with manipulative and Machiavellian personality types.

- A narcissist typically has a grandiose sense of self-importance. This could also be referred to as a sense of superiority. Beware those individuals who think that they are special because it often follows that they possess a sense of entitlement to whatever they please, and are willing to manipulate others to get it.
- They often have a distorted view of reality. The reason for this is that they cultivate fantasies to support their self-centered delusions because reality doesn't support them. Delusions of grandeur and unlimited power allow them to feel in control. The narcissist often fears reality, and any attempt to 'burst their bubble' should be avoided, as such attempts are often met with extreme emotions and potentially rage.
- An inability to empathize. Narcissists do not develop the ability to empathize with the emotions of those around them. As such, they have no issue with hurting people for personal gain. Frequently, they employ guilt and shame as weapons to use against you.

5 Tell-Tale Signs That You're Dealing With a Manipulator

Here are five specific behaviors to keep an eye out for:

1. **Deliberate button-pushing**. This may be in the form of a seemingly harmless banter or negative humor, but don't be fooled. Its real purpose is to demean you, providing the manipulator with a sense of superiority over you. For example, "What a lovely jacket! My mother also has one of those."

2. **Discomforting surprises.** If an individual seems to take pleasure in breaking bad news, beware of him/her.

3. **Sarcasm.** This is another method of veiling hostility towards you. By masking their nastiness with sarcasm, many manipulators think that they cannot be called out on it. This

category also includes repetitive teasing, often followed by a claim that they were "just kidding" or "only messing with you."

4. **Indirectly hurting you through someone or something that you hold dear.** This is another way to mask their truly manipulative identity. For example, a jealous and manipulative housemate might throw a red towel in the wash with your favorite white dress.

5. **Being controlling and possessive.** This applies especially to intimate and romantic relationships. Jealousy and possessive behaviors are a clear symptom of a toxic relationship. It's imperative to understand that you don't deserve to be locked away.

Real Life Examples

Here are a few practical examples of situations involving manipulations. Any encounter similar to these should be setting off alarm bells.

- There's someone close to you whose drama seems to revolve around. However, when it comes down to it, they never seem to be at fault. If someone is surrounded by upset, but always seemingly blameless, you should be suspicious.
- Word gets back to you that a potential manipulator has been discussing you behind your back, but when you confront them, they brush it off and try to reassure you with a pleasant smile. Beware the two-faced!
- Someone you spend time with frequently gives you cause to doubt yourself. It may simply be that this person is a manipulator, and cannot bear being wrong, so puts you down to compensate for their incorrectness.

Take Away Points

There are many ways to spot a manipulator. The main traits to keep an eye out for are:

- Lack of empathy
- Vicious humor
- Covertly hurting you

Narcissists are typically manipulative, so be aware of those with narcissistic traits.

The Manipulator in Action

"They know what makes us laugh, what makes us fearful, what excites us, what turns us off, and above all, what makes us vulnerable."

 - George Simon, Ph.D., an expert in character disorders

This chapter will explore in-depth some of the techniques most commonly employed by manipulators. As mentioned above, the purpose of these is not to teach you to manipulate others, but to make you aware of the methods used by those who would. You can't win a battle if you don't know who you're fighting, or what weapons they are using.

Gaslighting

The term 'gaslighting' comes from the title of the 1938 stage play Gaslight, (AKA Angel Street), in which a manipulative husband attempts to convince his wife that she is insane by manipulating small elements of her surroundings, insisting that she is misremembering things, and maintaining that she is delusional.

There are many ways that a manipulator can use gaslighting, but, in short, gaslighting is a form of manipulation that involves the sowing of doubt in your mind to the extent that you may begin to question your own memory, perception and/or sanity. Gaslighting is an extreme form of victimization that is most commonly seen in close couples.

Whilst this technique is most often seen in intimate and romantic relationships, where the two individuals have a solid understanding of one another's psychology, it can also occur in other settings, such as the workplace. An example of workplace gaslighting would be if a colleague convinced you to doubt the quality of your work, potentially by diverting conversations to weaknesses within it. Gaslighting is particularly detrimental when the perpetrator is in a position of power.

By constantly questioning you, a manipulator may lead you to feel that you are going crazy, that your memory is failing you, or that you are completely imagining things.

Another method of gaslighting is by twisting your words, and by applying a new meaning to what you said, despite knowing what you truly meant. For example, yesterday your partner promised to cook you a meal, but today they insist that you dreamed up the entire conversation.

Another more extreme example is in physically abusive relationships. There have been documented cases in which the abusive spouse maintains that they have never actually been violent in any way, forcing severe doubt into the victim's mind, and encouraging them to question their own mental health.

Gaslighting targets the victim's self-esteem, undermining them and the validity of their beliefs to the point that the victim themselves comes to believe that they are wrong. This may even lead to a form of Stockholm Syndrome, in which the victim becomes more attached to the manipulator, as they are so uncertain of reality that they have nowhere else to turn.

Psychological literature identifies three common forms of gaslighting:

1. **Hiding**. The manipulator hides objects from the victim in order to introduce an element of doubt into their psychological state, and possibly even blame themselves. It may be that this is an entry-level gaslighting, the first step towards instilling doubt in the victim.
2. **Changing**. The abuser may physically change something about the victim, such as a behavior or appearance. They are attempting to mold the victim to their design and, if the victim refuses, the manipulator may convince the victim that he/she is not good enough to fulfill their fantasy, and is therefore unworthy of their attention.
3. **Control**. This is common in jealous and overbearing partners. When the manipulator wants full control of the victim, it's likely that they will try to isolate and seclude them, limiting their interactions with family and friends whilst the manipulator gains pleasure from the sense of power and control that they feel.

In his book, State of Confusion: Political Manipulation and the Assault on the American Mind, Bryant Welch explores the extent to which the media, and especially politicians have used gaslighting to get their way. Therefore, this particular method of manipulation is not confined to intimate relationships but is broadly applicable to many aspects of everyday life.

Gaslighting is extremely prominent in American politics and journalism. Try watching a heated interview on Fox News, or something similar, to see how journalists employ manipulative word-twisting to make for a dramatic and confrontational segment of their show.

12 Ways Gaslighters Manipulate and Control Relationships

Writings on psychiatry typically conclude that severe gaslighting is highly detrimental to one's mental health, and frequently results in clinical depression. Here are some of the warning signs associated with gaslighting, so that you can avoid victimization:

1. The manipulator denies saying something altogether, even though you have proof and/or a vivid recollection of the event. They consistently deny this, until you begin to doubt your own memory.
2. The manipulator uses things and people that are close to you as a weapon against you. He/she may tell you that you aren't worthy of your partner, repeatedly, until you may just begin to believe them.
3. They highlight your negative traits. Nobody's perfect. We all have negative traits, but when someone focuses repeatedly on yours, it may be that they are trying to damage your ego, raising your self-consciousness.
4. They frequently tell blatant lies. They are bold and brash in their lying, maintaining a straight face, even when you have proof against them. This is a method of keeping you unsteady, off-kilter and questioning yourself.
5. They are persistent in their criticisms. Gaslighting often involves a gradual, longitudinal approach to emotional manipulation. It may even occur over the space of years. It may start small and build. Be aware of those who make

increasingly frequent put-downs.

6. General dishonesty. They say one thing and mean another. They don't follow through on promises, and you have several examples of this occurring.

7. They deliberately confuse you. Confusion is their friend and your enemy. It allows them to maintain a social edge over you, simply by making you unsure of your own thoughts.

8. They use positive reinforcement against you. We will discuss the positive reinforcement below.

9. They turn others against you. By telling others that you are imagining things, or even that you're crazy, the perpetrator strengthens their argument and weakens yours. They want you to be unsure of who you can trust, who you can turn to for clarification of what actually happened. They may even say "other people have noticed it too", "we're just concerned about you", or "we don't think you're quite right."

10. They tell you that everyone else is a liar. This encourages you to trust the gaslighter above all else and leaves you with few other options for where to turn when you need support.

11. They encourage your paranoia. They fuel the fire of doubt in your mind until it feels as though it is taking over.

12. A common method of gaslighting is to break you down, before building you back up again. This ensures that you are highly dependent on the manipulator and that you will always turn to them when your doubt hits a peak. Don't be fooled! They will tear you down again.

We will discuss methods of dealing with manipulators in general later on in this book, but, for now, here are a few things you might like to consider when you think you may be dealing with a gaslighter:

- **You need to be clear of who is gaslighting you and what methods they are using**. This will allow you to be certain, and such confirmation is essential to maintaining certainty in yourself.
- **Make notes** and keep a record of suspected attempts to undermine your mental health.
- **Meditation and mindfulness** allow for a certain clarity of mind that is difficult to maintain in the busy 21st-century lives that we lead. Even ten minutes per day could be beneficial, and it will help you to keep hold of the reality of your situation.
- **Discuss the gaslighter's accusations with your most trusted friends and family.** You can expect the truth from them. If you are being manipulated, they may be able to shed some light on the specifics and bring you some relief.
- If you feel that significant damage has been done to your mental health and your perspective of reality, then you should **consider seeking professional treatment** from a qualified therapist.
- Once you have overcome the manipulation and regained trust in yourself, it's time to consider yourself a survivor, no longer a victim.

Keep your ears pricked for these

To further prepare you, here are a few common gaslighting phrases, each of which serves the manipulator's needs in different ways.

"You're crazy. You need help/have issues."
"You're insecure/jealous."
"You're too sensitive/overreacting."
"I was only joking. You have no sense of humor."
"It's your problem, not mine."
"You're imagining things."
"I never said that."
"You're lying to me."
"Don't you remember?"
"Stop taking everything so seriously."
"What does that say about you?"

Although much of this information refers to preventative measures, such as identifying the gaslighter before they have had the opportunity to manipulate you, it's important to remember that, even if the damage has already been done, you can regain the self-confidence that the manipulator has stripped you of.

The Guilt Trip

Guilt-tripping is a covert intimidation tactic, a way for the manipulator to exploit your conscientiousness. It typically involves persuading you to feel guilty, usually by claiming that you are ungrateful, that you have it easy, or are to blame for a particular circumstance. The intention of this is generally to put you in a state of moral self-doubt.

A guilt tripper may try to make you feel responsible for something that is not necessarily your fault, in order to put you in a vulnerable and/or submissive position. It is generally considered to be a common form of passive aggression and may occur whether the victim is genuinely guilty or not. And it may even be nonverbal.

By reminding you of something painful, something that you did wrong or could have done better, the perpetrator gains the apparent moral high ground over you. The guilt tripper may then offer you an option to escape your guilt, proposing a way for you to right your wrongs, characteristically in a way that serves their needs. The intention is that you feel obliged to comply with their suggestion, so that you may free yourself of the guilt that they have imposed upon you.

When you refuse to comply with the guilt tripper's requests and desires, you may be met with antagonism, the silent treatment (discussed in more detail later), or general animosity. By doing this, they reinforce the seed of guilt that they have planted in your mind, forcing you to reconsider their request again and again.

Guilt-tripping has been observed in a variety of situations and relationships. The manipulator may be:

- A complete stranger.
- A close partner.
- A dear friend.
- A boss or colleague.
- Or even a parent/child. (Guilt trips are extremely dangerous to children, who are, tragically, one of the most common victims)

As with other techniques, guilt trippers have giveaways and tell-tale signs. The more aware you are, the better your psychological self-defense. Guilt trips are not the easiest psychological manipulation technique to spot, but here are some examples of warning signs to keep an eye out for:

- Passing responsibility. As their target, the buck will be passed to you. Beware of anyone trying to make you feel bad, even if it's for something you are actually responsible for... The potential guilt tripper may have an agenda of their own, beyond making you feel bad.
- The guilt tripper will likely nag you. They are repetitive in their accusations of responsibility. This is an attempt to grind you down.
- They may complicate matters. A guilt tripper's agenda may be forwarded by blowing your faults out of proportion, making mountains out of molehills and forcing you to consider your mistakes with greater weight than they in fact deserve.
- They drag up old instances where you were at fault. This is to provide them with more ammunition, making you feel guiltier still, whilst helping them to make their malicious and self-serving point.
- They may reference the occasions where they have helped you. This is a common trick that encourages you to consider yourself in their debt. They may begin sentences with phrases like "Remember when I did that thing for you...", "Don't you remember when I..." or "If it weren't for me...".

As far as manipulation techniques go, guilt-tripping is particularly hard to resist. This is because, at surface value, it seems as though the manipulator is being perfectly reasonable, and that you may indeed be at fault. Although methods for dealing with manipulators will be discussed in detail later on, here are some ways that might help you to deal specifically with a guilt tripper:

- Explain that, even if you go along with what they want, you are aware of their coercion and resent the fact that they would guilt-trip you.

- Tell them you understand how important it is to them that you do the thing they want you to, but that you don't appreciate the way that they are approaching the situation.

- Maintain a high level of self-esteem. This will make you a much harder target for the guilt tripper. The lower your self-esteem, the more likely you are to doubt yourself, and the easier it is for the perpetrator to convince you that you're in the wrong.

- Absolutely NEVER admit guilt when you are confident in your innocence. You need to be very honest with yourself about this, but never allow yourself to be persuaded of false guilt.

- Ask the guilt tripper to be more direct in their request. Explain that there's no need for coercion and that an up-front approach to problem-solving is far more likely to be successful.

- Try not to get caught up in a war of guilt. Maintaining the non-manipulative moral high ground is your very best option.

- It pays to be patient. The chances are that, at one time or another in life, you have also tried to guilt-trip someone, whether you meant to or not. Some social coercion stems from the subconscious, and it's worth remembering that we all have desires and that nobody is entirely innocent.

Passive Aggression

Whilst overtly aggressive behaviors are easier to spot, passive-aggressive behavior, often described as acting "catty," may be used by a manipulator who is trying to avoid direct confrontation. It is one of the sneakier methods they might use to get what they want. A passive-aggressive person may act consciously or subconsciously in their attempts to passively (indirectly) use subtle forms of aggression against you.

Whilst it's a term that we have all heard used before, many of us are unclear on exactly what it means. Simply, passive aggression is an attempt to be indirectly hostile towards you.

There are no guidelines as to what sort of person employs passive aggression. It may be a family member, partner, colleague or a complete stranger. In fact, the chances are that you have used it yourself at some point. It has also been suggested that certain medications can cause people to act with subtle aggression, so consider this when assessing a potential manipulator.

For the above reasons, it can be tricky to spot passive aggression, largely because it's such a significant part of everyday social interactions. So that you know what you're dealing with, here are a few instances of common passive-aggressive behaviors. Any of these should set off your now finely-tuned mental manipulator alarm:

- Claiming that they don't understand, when in fact they do. Playing dumb allows the manipulator to avoid any responsibilities. This is a common passive-aggressive strategy.
- It may be something as simple as a friend of a co-worker

who has failed to greet you when you know that normally they would. This gives you the impression that something is amiss, and maybe an attempt to bend you to their will.

- The silent treatment, whilst also mentioned elsewhere in this book, is another example of passive aggression. Being ignored in this way can be overt and obvious, such as your partner ignoring you because you said something to offend him, or it may be that the perpetrator claims their ignorance to be accidental.

- Subtle insults, often in the form of a backhanded compliment. It may be that you don't realize that the compliment was in fact an insult until the other person has already gone, but something about what they said wasn't as friendly as it seemed on the surface. For example, rather than saying your work is great, they may say that it's almost as good as your co-workers.

- Simple moodiness can be a method of disguising passive aggression. They may claim that they're just having a bad day, but you heard them talking with someone else and sounding perfectly chirpy. Again, you sense that something is amiss.

- Stubbornness. Some people are naturally stubborn. We've all met them, but others use an artificial stubbornness as something to hide behind, a way to punish you. There is usually little sense arguing with a person whose stubborn defenses are up.

- Passive-aggressive behavior can be as covert as simply under-performing. They won't fail to complete their task, but they will do it with minimum effort, for example, to spite the boss who set them their assignment. They may hide behind a mask of ambiguity, but they (and you) know exactly what they are doing!

Evidently, there are many forms of passive aggression. You should try to consider other behaviors that have more unpleasant underlying meanings than they seem at face value.

Now that you know what to keep a lookout for, here are a few methods that you can use when dealing with a passive aggressor:

1. Ignore them. Let the problem be theirs. This is also beneficial because they are often, on some level, aware of their manipulative behavior, and to call them on it may only serve to worsen their animosities. If you don't react, they may simply stop their behaviors.
2. Sometimes behavior cannot be ignored. They may have significantly offended you, and you feel that to remain silent would be failing to correct a genuinely nasty behavior. Try not to confront them. The best thing to do here would be to put some distance between you and them.
3. You could subtly try to make them aware of their behaviors if you think that they are not already consciously aware that they are using passive aggression. Don't try to make them admit anything, just share your thoughts about the possibility of their being indirect. Do this with tact and gentleness to try and avoid confrontation. Perhaps ask them if there's something else that could be bothering them and causing them to act in this way.

Intermittent Reinforcement

"The more infrequently the crumbs of love are offered, the more hooked you are. You become conditioned, like a rat in a cage."

-Unknown

Intermittent reinforcement, like positive reinforcement (discussed in greater depth below), is another manipulation method that uses conditioning to achieve the desired response. Conditioning is, basically, the use of a reward system to reinforce desirable behaviors.

Psychologists discovered that rewarding a rat regularly for behavior has diminishing returns, whereas rewarding the rat intermittently kept the subjects working harder for longer.

Intermittent reinforcement is the provision of rewards at irregular intervals. This method has been found, in studies of rats, primates, and humans, to yield the greatest results from the subject. In this case, the result is the victim's attempt to comply with the manipulator's desire.

Instead of, for example, a dog receiving a biscuit every time it executes a trick, it receives a biscuit intermittently, that is, irregularly. This encourages the dog to repeat the trick over and over (satisfying the manipulator) until the reward is given, seemingly at random.

Alarmingly, the same behavioral psychology theories apply to humans.

In the case of humans, the victim might be a lazy boyfriend, who leaves his clothes strewn across the bedroom floor every day. The manipulator, his girlfriend, rewards him intermittently with a kiss when he picks them up. Not every time, though. This encourages him to keep picking up his clothes until the next kiss (reward) is delivered.

Intermittent reinforcement is also employed by the tech giants that pull our strings as frequently as any other malicious entity. For example, your social media service determines that you are likely to log off soon. But it wants you to stay. It needs you to stay. So, shortly before it expects you to log off (having determined your usage patterns already), it delivers the "likes" that you have been waiting for regarding your holiday photographs. By feeding you these little bites of reinforcement at times that seem random (but are in fact determined by algorithms), they encourage you to stay. Creepy, aren't they?

So, that's one example of how intermittent reinforcement can be used for monetary gain by vast corporations. Can you avoid it?

Obviously, you could quit social media, but this writer doesn't expect you to do that; it's all simply too ingrained into real life. However, simply being aware of such an invasive manipulative practice gives you the edge on those who are not. When those endorphin-laced "likes" show up in your inbox, you can proceed to log off and come back to them at a time that suits you.

Yet another example is in gambling. The gambler is drip-fed just enough rewards to keep them playing, to keep them spending and hoping for that one get-rich-quick cash injection jackpot.

In relationships, intermittent reinforcement often comes in the form of attention and affection. When the manipulator treats their spouse coldly, they create fear in the victim, a fear of losing the relationship. When they intermittently reinforce, by offering affection in some way, the victim's hope is restored for a while, before being dashed once again. This serves as an extremely effective motivator for the victim to do everything they can to keep the relationship alive.

It's like the manipulator has control of the victim's dopamine supply, randomly throwing a reward whenever it suits them whilst the victim kneels, eagerly awaiting their next dose of pleasure.

Over time, intermittent reinforcement can be gradually and carefully elevated and ramped up to quite extreme levels. Some have even argued that, when considered over time, intermittent reinforcement is one of the most powerful dark psychological manipulation techniques known to man. It can potentially lead to obsessive and self-destructive behavioral patterns.

Manipulators, especially in the case of close, interpersonal relationships, may incorporate such **social isolation techniques** as:

- **The silent treatment**. A proven method dreaded by all. The manipulator withdraws communications as a punishment to the victim. The victim attempts to reform the communication pathway but is met by yet more silence.
- **The invisible treatment**. A stronger, but less common version of the silent treatment, in which the manipulator withdraws even more of their attention, refusing even to acknowledge the victim.

After being given one of the above treatments, the victim is flooded with pleasure and relief when the next dose of attention is delivered. This is the breaking down of hope, then sporadically reinforcing it.

The effects of intermittent reinforcement on the victim are quite varied, but, generally, symptoms include feeling needy, crazy or insecure. Never knowing where you stand in the relationship may cause you to act or feel in these ways. In intermittent reinforcement, the instability and uncertainty are the real tormentors.

Dealing with intermittent reinforcement is not the hardest thing to do; you need to break the cycle of dependence because intermittent reinforcements work just like an addiction.

Identifying when someone is using it against you, however, is extremely difficult. You could consider this relatively high-level manipulator spotting. Here are a few hints that you should find helpful:

- Someone close to you has suddenly become withholding of the thing that makes you happy. It may be affection, or it could come in just about any form. They drip-feed you this positive reinforcement, whereas they used to be generous with it.
- The unpredictability of someone's behavior is driving you crazy. Some days they seem to like their friendly selves, whilst other days they seem withdrawn and unfriendly.
- Look out for general inconsistencies in the perpetrator's mood and manner.

Bear in mind that the most common users of intermittent reinforcement are those closest to you, with the ability to grant and withhold pleasure.

Positive Reinforcement

Reinforcement is a long-standing behavioral psychology theory. It is a form of conditioning (reinforcing a particular desired behavior) through a system of punishment and rewards. It is a way of forcing another to learn a particular behavior and to repeat it.

Positive reinforcement specifically refers to the experimenter (potential manipulator) providing the subject (victim) with the desired reward each time they carry out the behavior that should be repeated. For example, when the dog does a trick, you give it a biscuit. It comes to associate the action with the reward, and is, therefore, more inclined to repeat the behavior (trick). This is known as operant conditioning.

Reinforcement of any type, including those discussed in previous sections of this book, can be applied to humans in both obvious and covert ways.

One example would be a gold star sticker reward system in a classroom; the children come to associate the behavior that the teacher desires with a form of reward (even when the reward has no actual value).

As mentioned, reinforcement can come in all shapes and sizes. For this reason, you may find a manipulator using reinforcement against you quite difficult to identify. In order to help you understand the variety of reinforcement methods that may be used, consider these examples of possible rewards:

- *Praise*. Simply congratulating you, giving you a little warm feeling of satisfaction can be enough to keep you repeating the desired behavior.
- *Money*. A financial reward is universally understood, though more common in certain cultures than in others. For example, giving a tip to a worker who did a good job, or pocket money to a child who has behaved well.
- *Charm*. Especially superficial charm. The manipulative charmer enjoys wrapping their victims around their fingers for full control.

- *Attention.* In the case of a close personal/romantic relationship, attention may serve as a reward that is either awarded for good behavior or withheld following undesirable behaviors. This is not the basis of a healthy relationship, and if you spot this dynamic within yours, you should probably consider speaking to your partner about it.
- *Gifts* of any sort. They could be physical gifts, or they could come in a less direct form, but a gift following the desired behavior may be a conscious attempt to reinforce that particular behavior. Keep this in mind, but don't become immediately suspicious of anyone who buys you flowers!
- A *smile.* Even a smile could be enough to manipulate your behavioral patterns, assuming you want the smiler to be happy. If you are suspicious of this practice, try looking at their eyes. We can often distinguish a false smile from a genuine one by considering the smiler's eyes.

It should be noted that positive reinforcement may occur naturally in a relationship and that it is not necessarily malicious. It can even be part of a perfectly healthy relationship, providing that things don't go too far. If you find yourself craving for your next hit of reinforcement, maybe it's time to ask whether your actions make you happy, or if you're just chasing an endless breadcrumb trail of gifts and smiles for no real reason.

Using your own judgment is the best thing to do here; consider things on a case by case basis, and know that some relationship counselors even recommend an amount of positive reinforcement to encourage a cooperative relationship.

A Word About Negative Reinforcement

You, as someone who is beginning to understand how psychological manipulation can work, should also consider negative reinforcement. Negative reinforcement is the opposite of positive reinforcement but is still another way to influence behaviors. In this case, it involves removing a punishment (rather than giving a reward) to reinforce a behavior.

An example of negative reinforcement is a husband willingly doing the dishes (the desired behavior), because he knows that his wife will nag him (a form of punishment) if he leaves them in the kitchen sink.

In summary, reinforcement can occur naturally or maliciously in obvious or covert styles. You should be aware of the possibilities, but careful not to jump to any conclusions regarding peoples' motives.

Invalidation

Invalidation is a method of demeaning a person by ignoring or rejecting their thoughts and feelings. Such a technique may be used by manipulators who seek to wear you down or instill self-doubt in an attempt to make the victim feel worthless.

Invalidation keeps the victim at a distance by reducing the value of their thoughts and feelings and maybe just one part of an ongoing psychological war between manipulator and victim. Like gaslighting, invalidation is another method that can be used to make the victim feel as though they are losing their faculties when they are in fact perfectly sane.

Invalidation is a particularly dirty manipulation technique, as it is directly harmful to the victim. Being invalidated can worsen self-esteem issues and make a recovery from depression or anxiety much more difficult.

It can occur in various forms. It may be rejecting the value of someone's perceptions, mocking their feelings, or outright ignoring someone's contributions to a conversation. This leads the victim to feel under-valued, and in turn, diminishes their confidence.

Whilst invalidation is extremely commonplace in all social situations (workplace, family, romantic partner, etc.), it is extremely unhealthy. It may be that the manipulator is completely unaware that they are doing it. It may be that they simply lack empathy. It may even be that you are the manipulator, and hadn't realized that, by ignoring or consistently rejecting a friend or colleague, you are causing them significant mental anguish.

The terrible truth is that invalidation has become commonplace, acceptable behavior in modern society.

As mentioned, some may use invalidation without knowing, but others would deliberately weaponize it for any number of reasons. They may envy you, and so seek to reduce you to the level that they perceive themselves to be on. They may feel that, by invalidating others, they gain a competitive edge in terms of social interaction.

Simply, invalidation may be perceived as a lack of empathy in the abuser. Once again, this raises the issue of narcissism, which is often characterized by a lack of empathy.

We all have emotional needs, and we all seek to satisfy them. When a manipulator invalidates our needs, he/she undermines them. We feel that our needs are unimportant, that we perhaps complain too much, or even that we are unloved.

Research has even found that prolonged emotional invalidation can lead a victim to emotional suppression, i.e., repressing feelings and inhibiting emotional thoughts. Furthermore, emotional suppression is strongly associated with high levels of psychological distress and dissatisfaction.

Invalidation doesn't have to be vocal, but more often than not it is, so here are a few examples of statements that may be intended to invalidate you:

- Must we talk about this again?
- You're taking it too seriously.
- We already spoke about this.
- You don't even know how lucky you are.
- Get over it. / Cheer up. / Stop whinging.
- You take everything so personally.
- Don't act so seriously.
- Don't be ridiculous.
- Don't be so judgemental.
- Are you joking?
- You're just tired. / You're just hungry.
- It's not a big deal.
- You ought to be thankful.
- Just forget about it all.
- Stop imagining things.
- You're sounding crazy.

As mentioned, invalidation isn't necessarily always verbal. For example, the silent treatment could be employed to make you feel that your previous comment wasn't worthy of a response, or by an abuser simply rolling their eyes, you might feel that you're undervalued or that your contribution was stupid. By showing impatience or boredom in their body language, the invalidator makes you feel undervalued. There are many ways that invalidation could occur, and you should use your imagination to ensure that you are aware of all possibilities.

In the case that you feel invalidated by your partner in a close relationship, you should raise the point with them gently. Explain that you don't feel that your emotions are valued by them, and help them to identify their problematic behaviors by highlighting a few of the undermining phrases that they use. Keep in mind that their behavior may be accidental.

The best solution is to replace the invalidation with genuine validation. Pay attention to one another's feelings, and try reversing some of the above statements to help you or the perpetrator to be more positive in the way that they receive your feelings.

Triangulation

"Never let the other person use absence, or create pain and conflict, to keep you, the seduced, on tenterhooks."

- Robert Greene, The Art of Seduction

Triangulation is another manipulation method that is designed to make the victim seem insecure and is especially applicable to close personal relationships. It involves the manipulator bringing a third person into the relationship equation, causing the victim to feel doubtful about the solidity and future of the relationship. By doing this, the manipulator has not only put you on the back foot and forced you to consider a future in which the relationship fails, but they have also made you considerably more eager to please them.

A clear example would be if your partner flirting with someone else. This action may be to deliberately cast doubt upon their feelings for you and encourage you to try and please them to regain your status in the relationship.

What's more, if you confront a manipulator who is using triangulation, you may even find yourself being blamed for the issue! They may openly claim that the problem is not with their behavior, but a symptom of your insecurity.

You should seek to bring your relationship out into the open. You both need to be on the same page, where you both feel a sense of security and stability. Also, consider how much you would actually want to be with a person who might use a manipulation tactic as vicious as this one.

Trust. Is. Essential.

Hey!

Sorry to interrupt. I just wanted to check-in and ask if you're enjoying the book?

I'd love to hear your thoughts!

Reader reviews are the lifeblood of any author's career. Many readers don't know how much they help an author.

So I would be incredibly thankful if you could take **just 60 seconds** to leave a quick review on Amazon, even if it's just a sentence or two!

» Click here to leave a brief review on Amazon.«

Thank you and I look forward to reading your review.

P.S. Leave me a little message as I personally read each and every review!

Lying

Lying, by its definition, is deliberately presenting falsehood as the truth… but of course, you already knew that.

It is still, however, important to consider why the manipulator lies. There are many approaches to lying, some of which tie into the manipulation methods that we have already discussed. The manipulator's motive to lie is something that you should always consider when you become suspicious, or when you catch someone in a lie.

Ask yourself "what are they getting out of this lie?"

Some are better at lying than others, and the best liars are extremely good at it. They can look us in the eye with a reassuring smile and tell us something that is entirely untrue, yet we believe it all the same.

There are many approaches to lying, and a lie does not always come in the simple form of an untrue statement. It may be that the lie is actually a half-truth, making it even easier to believe. Also, consider how a manipulator may deliberately withhold information; the absence of truth is a lot easier to justify than an outright lie, yet it has a similar effect.

It's important that we are aware of liars, and that we are skeptical when presented with information that we just don't know to be true. When this happens, consider the following questions:

- What might be their motive for lying about this? Is there anything in it for them?

- Has this person ever lied to me before? Do I generally consider them trustworthy?

- Do I have any evidence to the contrary of what they are saying?

- Don't get too caught up in doubting everything you hear. People are not all innately cruel. Sometimes, we have to take things at face value, and to become too wrapped up in skepticism can lead to an unhealthy, paranoid state of mental being.

Love Bombing

"Any halfway-clever devil would decorate the highway to hell as beautifully as possible."
- Criss Jami

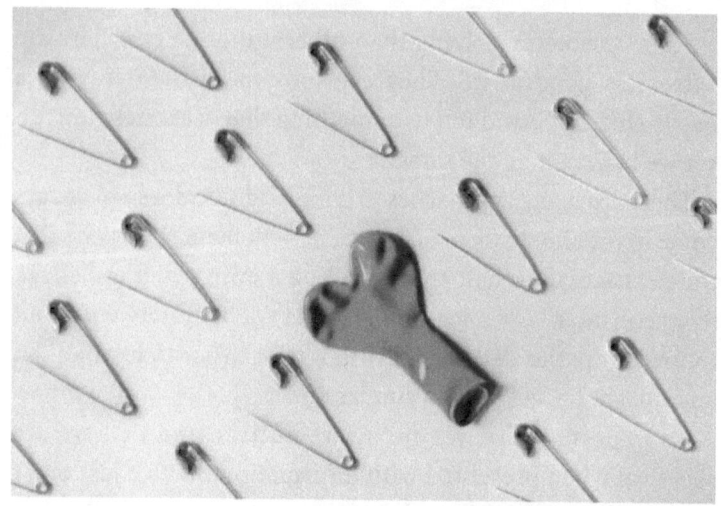

Whilst general flattery has its place in many methods of psychological manipulation, love bombing is an attempt to specifically influence an individual by bombarding them with positivity. It has various uses, of which psychological manipulation is just one.

It has been used by cults and lovers alike and identified by psychologists as a potentially potent method of manipulation. By overwhelming someone with 'love', attention and affection, a feeling of unity and a co-dependence (whether healthy or not) can be established.

Love bombing is employed by narcissists often to win your confidence. How could such an overly positive and endearing person mean you any harm? Beware of those who are overly flattering, as they may be pulling your strings.

Love bombing is a bit of a Trojan horse. At first, it feels good, and that is very much the purpose. To put you at ease, to make you more open, or to win your affection. But, be assured that soon enough it will stop feeling so good and the narcissist will get their way.

It has also been suggested that social media worsens love bombing, and similar methods of abuse because the perpetrator has almost constant communication with the victim.

Examples of behaviors that may indicate love bombing or over-flattering behaviors include the following:

- The potential narcissist showers you with gifts. They must be after something, and they think they can win you over with things.
- The romantic partner who texts you relentlessly, their attention seemingly always on you, but you suspect that their mind is elsewhere.
- Your relationship is moving uncomfortably fast. They tell you that they have loved no one like they love you. You are meant to be together and they have never been more certain of anything.
- It may be that a colleague constantly compliments your work above anyone else's, and they do this far too frequently.

There are various reasons for why a manipulator may love bomb you:

- Their personality is lacking, so they compensate with material objects.

- They feel guilty and are flattering for forgiveness.

- As a method of baiting and switching. They are getting you to lower your defenses.

- They want to build up your image of them. They want to be seen as eternally loving and probably quite wealthy.

Be warned that there's a fine line between love bombing and

normal, healthy affection, so be careful not to misinterpret someone's love for manipulation.

That said if it begins to feel more like stalking than affections... you might just have a narcissist on your hands.

Recap

We have now explored some of the logistics of psychological manipulation, the practical techniques. Here are the main takeaway points from this chapter:

There are many forms of manipulation. The most common include:

1. Gaslighting is leading people to doubt themselves
2. Guilt-tripping is exploiting someone's conscientiousness
3. Positive/Negative reinforcement is a form of conditioning
4. Intermittent reinforcement is a powerful but unpredictable motivator
5. Invalidation is the dismissal of someone else's thoughts or feelings
6. Lying comes in all shapes and sizes

There are other subcategories within these that encompass common techniques such as the silent treatment, love bombing and triangulation.

Dealing With Manipulators

"Love comes when manipulation stops; when you think more about the other person than about his or her reactions to you. When you dare to reveal yourself fully. When you dare to be vulnerable."

- Joyce Brothers

Whilst there are as many approaches to dealing with manipulation as there are approaches to manipulating another, this chapter will highlight some methods and tactics that you may use in the case that you find yourself being exploited through one of the methods discussed in the previous chapter.

The good news is that the root of the problem is often within the manipulator themselves, though they would have you believe otherwise. It frequently stems from a feeling of inadequacy or a lack of emotional intelligence and empathy. It may be that the manipulator is afraid of failure or in need of constant validation and that the only way they can achieve this is by stepping on others.

This means that the manipulator has vulnerabilities and that their nastiness may simply be part of a cold exterior that is designed to propel them towards their self-serving goals. It would be helpful to remember this when dealing with a confrontational manipulator, but not to exploit these weaknesses; to do so would be to lose the moral high ground of the situation.

Some methods mentioned here will be relevant to specific forms of manipulation, whilst others are more of a broad approach to how to manage people around you with toxic and narcissistic personalities.

Remember, a confrontation with a manipulator is a delicate matter and must be handled as such.

How To Disarm a Manipulator

Whilst, as previously mentioned, many manipulators will go to great lengths to avoid confrontation, it is likely that their actions will culminate in, at the very least, a heated discussion. Here are a few ideas to help you deal with this encounter:

- Remain calm and controlled. Do not lose your temper. This is absolutely essential when it comes to maintaining your moral high ground. If you start raving at someone about how manipulative they are, you will soon find yourself being taken less seriously. A calm and calculated, but emotionally present approach is advisable.
- Avoid personal blame. You are not the problem, and you should not allow the manipulator to turn the tables on you. As mentioned earlier, manipulators are often keen to pass the blame onto their victims. This serves two needs. Firstly, it puts the victim in a difficult, uncertain position of doubt. Secondly, it frees them of any blame, allowing them to proceed in their wily, manipulative ways.
- Keep control of the conversation. Try to take the conversational lead by asking them questions, rather than allowing

them to probe you. This also serves two needs; it shows them that you are not to be trifled with, that you are willing to stand up for yourself and are in control, and secondly, by probing them, you can get closer to the root of the problem, digging out the facts and discarding their lies.

- Call them out on their behavior. There are some (above) examples of situations when this is specifically not advised, but sometimes, a bold and simple approach is favorable. Don't do this with any aggression. Try to phrase the inquisition not as an accusation of them, but as a suggestion as to the cause of their behaviors.
- Walk away. By perpetuating your relationship with the manipulator, you just add fuel to their fire. If you are not interacting with them, and you have no need to interact with them in the future, then simply leave. Obviously, this is not advisable in the case of a partner, friend or family member, but if the manipulator is a relative stranger, what's to lose?
- Deal with the questionable behavior as soon as possible. Don't allow yourself to get used to it. If you let them get away with whatever it is that they shouldn't be doing, they will almost certainly try it again and again. This is especially true in the case of those with narcissistic personality disorders.

Call a spade a spade, but don't call a narcissist a narcissist. Be upfront and truthful and honest in your conversation with the manipulator. Let them know how their actions affect you, and how that makes you feel.

BUT, be careful to avoid angering them or directly accusing them. Although they seem cold and cruel in their actions, they may just be behaving manipulatively because they feel insecure in themselves. Remember this, but don't weaponize it.

How To Break Free And Keep The Manipulator At a Distance

Here are a few key tips to help you avoid this happening:

- **Do not consider revenge.** Nothing good will come of it. The narcissist enjoys drama and manipulative warfare, so it's advisable to not give them the satisfaction. Just take comfort in the knowledge that you blew their disguise, identified them as a manipulator, and walked away from them.
- **Cut all communications.** If a narcissist has been particularly damaging to your psyche, you may consider cutting all contact absolutely. Block their number, avoid the places that you know they frequent, and try to keep distinctly separate social circles.

- **Trust your own judgment and do what you know is best for you.** This may mean ending a particularly toxic relationship, but deep down you know that it's the only way to get out from underneath your oppressive partner. Of course, you shouldn't make any rash decisions, especially when in a state of frustration. Weigh up the pros and cons of your relationship, and objectively assess any issues before confronting your partner about them.
- **Seek professional help.** Psychiatry has numerous methods of rebuilding your self-confidence and helping you to heal the wounds. If you feel that any damage that may have been done is significant, or if you're struggling to deal with things on your own and your loved ones haven't been much help, you should consider this.
- **Come to terms with what has happened.** Maybe the manipulator fooled you. Maybe they got the better of you. Maybe they hurt you in some way or did some psychological damage whilst they took you for a ride. But you have come through the other side. Now is the time to stop considering yourself a victim, and to consider yourself a survivor... Congratulations!

Some Narcissist-Specific Advice

As mentioned, many manipulators are narcissists and vice versa. Here are a few practical pointers for when it comes to dealing with your narcissistic manipulator.

1. Understand exactly who they are. Remember that narcissism is part of them. It's not impossible that they may change, but it could take a great deal of your energy to

make them do so.

2. If you find yourself being drawn into their web of neediness, take some time to yourself and remember that it's not your job to fix this person.

3. Set boundaries that maintain your privacy and personal space. Narcissists often have a sense of entitlement, to you and to your things. As soon as they overstep, be sure to put them in their place, as an invasive behavior allowed to go unpunished will almost always result in a repeat offense.

4. Expect resistance. They will push back against your boundaries. This is the real test because it's time for you to stand your ground and stick to your (metaphorical) guns!

5. Understand that the narcissist themselves may need professional help. People with Narcissistic Personality Disorder often have overlapping disorders such as substance abuse. These people don't need beating into submission. They need coaxing into getting treatment. Try gently questioning their well-being and checking that they are feeling okay, or explaining that you are concerned about them.

6. Above all of the advice in this section, remember that narcissists are still people; they are individuals and each one is different. Therefore, you cannot simply approach any manipulator or narcissist in a generic manner. Your confrontation must be tailor-made to suit them.

Recap

Here are a few concise points for you to take away from this chapter. Try to keep them in mind whilst deciding how to address the problem of your manipulator.

1. Keep hold of your moral high ground.
2. A short temper is your enemy.
3. Be honest, but not confrontational.
4. Once you have made your decision, stick with it.
5. Overcome the damage done, and accept that it was a learning experience.

Conclusion

The purpose of this book is to provide you with some insight into how a manipulator may exploit you, in the hope that you may avoid some psychological trauma in the future.

Now that we have covered a range of psychological manipulation techniques, looked at who the manipulators are and why they do it, and learned that the root of the problem most often lies within the liars themselves, you should feel better equipped to face those people who might seek to do you harm. You now have the tools at your disposal that allow you to identify a manipulator, regardless of their methods, and to deal with the issue appropriately.

Keeping the main points of this book fresh in your mind will help you to identify and deal with manipulators. To help you do this, here is a list of the 12 key takeaway points that you can use to refresh your memory at any time. It's advisable that you refer back to the relevant section when you are suspicious of a potential manipulator.

1. Firstly, we learned that manipulators do indeed exist and that there are plenty of them. They come in many forms and, because of this, it's important that we educate ourselves on how they operate.

2. We then explored exactly the sort of people that are prone to using social manipulation. We discussed the dark triad and narcissism, learning that the manipulator is often an unwell individual with deeply seeded issues of their own.

3. A manipulator's motivation can be anything, but they often control freaks with little empathy and are likely to target those they perceive as vulnerable.

4. We then looked at the common traits of a manipulator and narcissists. You may find it helpful to refresh your memory of these before applying your new skills to real-life situations (Chapter 2).

5. The first of the main manipulation techniques that we looked at was gaslighting. This involves the manipulator sowing seeds of doubt in the mind of the victim, to the extent that they may question their own mental health.

6. Guilt-tripping is when the manipulator attempts to exploit your conscientiousness.

7. Passive aggression is a discreet but damaging way of oppressing you and your ideals. It comes in all shapes, like manipulators themselves.

8. Intermittent reinforcement is the random presentation of rewards. It keeps you working hard and long at trying to please the manipulator.

9. Positive reinforcement is less malicious. It involves rewarding the desired behavior in the hope that this will lead to it being repeated.

10. We also briefly touched upon triangulation (in intimate relationships) and, more generally, lying.

11. In the third chapter, we explored the best ways to deal with a manipulator, learning that confrontation is best avoided, but may occasionally be unavoidable.

12. It's best to keep a distance and assess the damage, before moving on with your life.
13. All of the above is important information, but most significantly, you must remember to be your own person and to act for your own reasons. To be a puppet, dancing at the end of someone else's strings, whether they are held by your partner or your government, is quite simply no life at all.

Thank you for reading.

Now, remember to use your powers wisely.

Don't Forget Your FREE Gift!

* * *

As a way of saying thank you for your purchase, I'd like to give you a **Free** gift!

The Cruelest Face of "Love" Revealed' is your essential quick-start guide to help you detect & escape high-conflict personalities in your life.

»CLICK HERE to download your FREE Guide now!«

*** The offer expires in 24 hours so go ahead click the link and grab your copy now!

Understand how they hook you so insidiously and deceptively, so you can stop feeling guilty about missing red flags.

» Click Here to Get Your 100% Free Bonus Now!«

II

How To Analyze People: The Revealing Power Of Facial Expressions

Read People Accurately and Spot any Subtle Social Cues, Hidden Emotions or even Potential Deception via Nonverbal Behavior

Introduction

I want to thank you and congratulate you for downloading the book, *Analyze people: The revealing power of facial expressions*.

This book contains proven steps and strategies on how to analyze people with the aid of facial expressions.

Your ability to analyze people has a great impact on the manner in which you shall deal with them. As you get to understand the other person's feelings, you get to adapt your message and begin communicating in a way that yields the maximum results possible. This is also essential as it tends to avoid the possibility of causing chaos among the two of you.

Think of a situation where somebody is angry over a certain matter but manages to hide it. On your part, you are unaware of this anger issue and begin to make jokes around the same. As much as your friend could have kept you in the dark regarding the problem, you making fun of it could result in them being infuriated and eventually all that anger bursts out of them.

There are different strategies you could follow in analyzing people. You may decide to listen to their words, take a look at hand gestures or even analyze their facial expressions. You may decide to pay attention to deviations (inconsistencies) in the gestures and words used by someone. Of all of these strategies, facial expression seems to be the most effective one. Most people may devise ways to control their words and actions, but they tend to have difficulty controlling what their faces say. The face simply never lies. It is similar to a little child lying to you that she hasn't taken candy but you can see sugary marks on their mouth.

Due to the amazing power of facial expressions to always reveal the truth, this book concentrates on helping you read someone's face and reveal the underlying truth in whatever they tell you. It aims at equipping you with this essential people-reading skill so that you are never deceived again.

Whether you are dealing with your partner whom you suspect of cheating, or a work colleague who might have tried to undercut you in a deal, the people analysis skill will help you get your facts right. And even as you gain the skills to read other people, there are times you personally want to share a different message with the others while at the same time making sure that your facial expressions do not give you away. Maybe you want to encourage your child to face a particular matter but you personally have your doubts. It is important that you also have what it takes to manage your personal facial expressions. This book will show you how to do that.

Thanks again for downloading this book, I hope you enjoy it!

The Essence of Analyzing People's Facial Expression

People are an open book. If you pay a keen attention to what they do and look at their facial expressions as they speak, you are likely to get a better picture of their attitudes and personalities. It is important to analyze people as this gives you an upper hand in different situations. This chapter demonstrates the different reasons as to why you should analyze people.

Helps strike healthy friendship

A common misconception about the analysis of people is that it may lead to trust issues. That is entirely untrue. When you make analysis of people prior to even becoming friends, you get to know them better and can thus form healthy friendships. You know their likes and dislikes, and can even tell if they are genuine or not. With these facts, individuals who know how to analyze people will always get into helpful and healthy friendships and relationships. You do not want to get into relationships and friendships that will lead you to being taken advantage of. The only way to guarantee that is not to just take in the words said by the other person but to also look at their facial expressions and tell whether the two agree.

Helps find a common ground

If you know how to analyze people, you can put that skill into arriving at a common ground. This is a skill that you will not just use with a few people. It can also be used while delivering vital speeches to various audiences. As you say something, you gauge what their reactions are through people's analysis skill. When you realize that you have gone too far, you can backtrack slightly so that you all get to a common understanding. Getting to a common understanding means being at a position that is neutral for both of you, hence chances of getting into confrontations are minimized.

Helps speak in a language understandable to your audience

When you know how to analyze people, you can tell when they understand what you are saying and when they don't. At such times, you can easily see when whatever you have been saying hasn't been understood, even if the other person doesn't tell you that. For example, as a teacher, you could see from your student's faces that they are lost and require proper clarification. Similarly, as a parent, you may give instructions to your children but that doesn't mean they will understand whatever you said right away. Through the people analysis skills, you can gauge whether your communication style is being understood by the other person or whether you need to change your mode of message delivery.

Makes you dependable for advises

Your friends are bound to get into trouble from time and again with their boyfriends or girlfriends. Because you know how to analyze people, you can listen to their side of the story while analyzing them too and also get to interact with their partners before giving advice. People tend to reveal more with their facial expressions. You can analyze these to get the hidden message behind their words. The advice you give is more likely to be genuine and helpful. They are based on facts rather than assumptions, hence helpful to the person asking for your advice. Even if your advice would not be followed to completion as you would have wanted, time will prove that you were right. That goes a long way in solidifying your position as a dependable person for advice.

You are always prepared

If you know how to analyze people, you will always be prepared for outcomes that would have otherwise been surprising. Whether you are getting ready for a meeting with the board of directors, or your juniors at work made a catastrophic mistake that they are trying to hide, you can analyze them and know it. We live in a world where however possessing information has the upper hand. When you analyze members of your team, you are able to collect the information without them even knowing it. In case they were planning anything that isn't favorable to you, you can undo it prior to its occurrence. Let's say your boyfriend or girlfriend has been acting weirdly in recent days but they still tell you everything is fine. You could use your analysis skills to find out that they are actually cheating and even have plans to break up with you! They may think that their plans are well hidden but in real sense you already have the facts and just decided to play along. When they eventually decide to come out of the hiding and drop the bombshell, it won't be much of a bombshell to you.

It makes you more considerate

The fact that you analyze people gets you to understand why they may act in certain ways. You develop some sense of protection towards others, a protectionist behavior that the average person may not have. If you are the boss at your workplace or in any other organization and conflicts are brought to you, you will want to first analyze the conflicting persons prior to decide. The ability to listen to all the people will not be motivated by you having too much time but by the desire to analyze all so that you do not end up making the wrong decision. During the analysis, important information is revealed to you like what would have actually made people to act in such and such a manner. Thus, as you start making the final decision, you will put all these facts into consideration. This is in contradiction to individuals who make decisions based on what they hear. The decisions of such individuals could even be biased and may end up punishing the wrong person. As a person with people analysis skills, punishment is not within your scope because you know sometimes people act not out of their will but out of a background force. This force is only revealed to you when you analyze them.

You get really smart

Not to brag but knowing how to analyze people makes you really smart. From the many years of doing this, you wire your brains to think in a certain manner that the brains of other people do not. The process has also led you to know the many different types of people on our planet and can form topics that anchor well with these. You form well formulated opinions on topics and can't wait to speak them out. You are the kind of a person who can deliver an electrifying speech on different occasions with various audiences. All you have to do is analyze the audience and choose the direction in which your topic should move. Furthermore, the people analysis skills empower you to stimulate anyone's brain. Thinking, talking, discussing and conversing are your erogenous zones and anyone can tap into those in a stimulating way. Having understood the other person, you know what you can say to get them stimulated and what to avoid as it could lag them behind.

Facial Communication for Personal Happiness

Effective facial expression communication skills are of benefit to any person at any stage of their life. These are the kinds of skills that are needed in personal life and in professional life as well. The constant reminder since childhood that you need to sharpen your communication skills wasn't in vain. That's because your elders at that time knew what communication skills can do for your life. Now that you are old enough, you should have a better understanding as to why facial communication is such a crucial issue in human relations.

Improving your ability to communicate with your facial expressions can tremendously benefit different spheres of your life. You should expect to increase your happiness, confidence and successful social interaction.

Enhance opportunities for personal growth

When you increase your ability to facially communicate effectively, you open up more avenues for your personal growth. People are happier when they have a sense of improvement rather than stagnation. Individuals who have these strong communication skills have better leadership abilities including the motivation of family members at home or subordinates at work. From the perspective of self-maintenance, the communication skills are essential in the management of stress. When you have good communication skills, you can properly share with your therapist whatever is bothering you and he/she will be able to help you accordingly.

Facial communication skills also make you assertive, meaning that you can effectively take charge of conversations or situations, bringing about meaningful conclusions. You do not want to keep revolving around a matter for too long as doing so is equivalent to wasting time, which has zero benefit to your personal growth.

With improved communication skills, you are able to meet a partner or make new friends. Due to the strong command on your communication, you carry yourself in a confident manner, attracting admiration from others. It allows you to project some gregarious and charismatic personality which most people love associating with. These advances in personal growth goes a long way in improving your networking skills, hence more opportunities for your social life and professional progression. The state of our world today requires you to have different kinds of connections in order to be more competitive. Your ability to ingratiate yourself with company top management may see you get more responsibilities, higher pay and increased chances to climb the social ladder.

Physical communication consists of facial expressions, hand gestures, fidgeting and eye movement, all of which constitute major parts of a communication. Many also consider this to be the hardest form of communication to monitor and control. People tend to be focused mainly on what they are hearing and saying such that they forget to pay attention to what their physical movements are saying. If you can be able to control that, you will have an upper hand in the conversation. This is something that an effective communicator is able to do and in the long run see their personal lives grow further.

With effective communication, you will be able to earn a diploma, find your dream job, master the art of persuasion, and increase your visibility and reach. All these factors are associated with personal growth and bring one immense happiness.

Listening to underlying needs

Talking of underlying needs, it is vital that you be able to identify these needs in others as well. During most negotiations, it is typical for people to commonly pay attention to the demands being made by the other side. However, what they should actually focus on is the other person's unexpressed desires and underlying needs.

Given that we all have unique needs, it is possible to satisfy several people without losing. All you have to do is make use of your effective communication skills to understand the underlying needs involved and satisfy them. Do not be hindered by what the other person is saying. Your concentration ought to be on the needs. What could be any happier ending in a negotiation than for all of you to end up at a win-win situation?

Imagine a situation where your family is planning a vacation. This is supposed to be a happy negotiation but you get into a deadlock as you can't seem to settle on the final vacation destination. Your son wants to go to the Rocky Mountains while your spouse wants Texas. The differences may seem irreconcilable at the start but if you open up the communication lines and look beyond the demands, you will see that there are needs which can be met jointly. From gentle inquiry, you may realize that your wife just needs a place that is warm and has tennis facilities while your son just wants to see mountains. Having learnt this, you will be able to see that a resort in Colorado can meet these needs.

Effective communication for happy relationships

When you are happy in your relationship, you are bound to be happy overall. Most of the time the sadness that surrounds our work life or relations with our friends can be associated directly with differences in our relationships. Many people tend to carry their arguments with their spouse to other spheres of their lives. Thus, it is logical to conclude that if you can establish a happy relationship, you will be happier. That is achievable through healthy communication.

A healthy communication is a kind of communication in which you listen to your partner speak before responding accordingly. You do not engage in undue shouts against each other. Rather, you are patient enough to let the other finish telling their side of anything while you give them your undivided attention. Effective communicators know how to do so.

Always remember that listening is the most important communication skill in your relationship. As the other person is speaking, do not daydream or get lost into thinking about what to say next. When you listen, you will be able to give appropriate feedback, making your partner happy and in the long run have a satisfactory relationship.

How To Tell if Someone's Faking

In chapter 3, you will learn how to decode facial expressions but before that, it is paramount that you have a strong grasp on how people can hide these expressions. When you have this understanding, you are empowered to tell if someone is trying to create different perceptions in your mind from what their words are saying. This chapter seeks to enlighten you on that.

Why do people try to hide their facial expressions?

There are a number of reasons as to why people choose to hide their facial expressions. For some, it is a way suppressing their emotions towards a given matter. As much as their words portray a particular image in your brain, it is their wish that you do not get to see their actual emotions on the same subject. For example, you may be holding a conversation with a potential partner who likes you but they are afraid to let you know that – maybe because they are too shy or unwilling to be the first ones to reveal that. Because of their unwillingness to express their emotions, they could try to fake their facial expressions. In such a case, it is up to you to discover that on your own. You have to look closely at their faces as they speak to you so as to get their actual feelings. You never know if it could be the only thing that leads you to finding one true love!

Some people have just too much ego that they wouldn't allow their facial expressions to be shown. When clearly a particular matter has hurt them and that they are undergoing immense pain inside, their big egos would not let them reveal such details. These are the kinds of people who suffer in silence and within a couple of days, you may get information that they did something more harmful – suicide for example.

There is also this category of people who hide their facial expressions, not because they want to do so, but because they just do not know how to solve negative emotions. As negativity builds up from the inside and starts to show in the face, they soon devise ways to hide any form of negative expressions to lock you out from analyzing them. They want to look happy when in real sense they are sad. They want you to see that they are having a good time but in reality there is a sickness or school fees issue that has been stressing them for months now. We all know that negative emotions can lead to frowning on one's face, which essentially makes them not so approachable or appealing. Thus, in an attempt to retain their attractiveness, they conceal any form of negative facial expression which would have otherwise confronted them.

In other cases, some people may hide their facial expressions just so as to please. These are the people who believe in the philosophy that what you do not know cannot hurt you. Their idea is that when they keep some information from you, you may still have a happy life. Thus, when they speak to you, they will struggle to build a certain kind of facial expression which conveys the message that all is well while in real sense that is further from the truth. Let's say for example one of your best friends gets some bad news from the doctor that they have cancer and that they have only a few years with you. They love you so much and know how much such news could be devastating to you. In order to save you all the pain, they may choose to struggle with the pain on their own, believing that provided you do not know about it, you will have a happy life. Whenever they tell stories with you, they will do their best not to let you inside. From their facial expressions, they will be smiling for you whereas only they know the agony they are experiencing. You have the responsibility of decoding this so that you get the message they are trying to lock inside.

5 Signs someone is being fake: How to tell they are faking facial expressions

1. Taking deep breath

This is a technique that seems to be universal amongst all people who express untrue facial expressions. You will often see them appear to be unrelaxed and continuously breathe in and out heavily in the midst of their explanations over a matter you just asked. Because they know that for you to believe the facial expression they just wore to impress you, they have to appear calm. That is what the deep breathes are meant to do – take in more oxygen so that they can recollect their composure and be cool. If you are not keen enough on the breathing pattern, their faces may appear calm to you and succeed in the deception.

2. Putting up a fake smile

A smile never says that someone is happy at all times. Someone who smiles and has a bubbly look on their face can win hearts and affection. As a result, many assume that with just the right smile, they will be able to hide their feelings like anger or sadness. But a fake smile will always be fake. It may convince some people at the first glance but a keen individual will soon realize this smile is fake. How well you know the individual could guide you into distinguishing between the smile they just put up and their real happy smile. But even if you do not know them that well, their inability to sustain the smile will eventually prove it fake.

3. Trying not to supporting the head

There is something about 'cooked' facial expressions that makes the head heavy. A droopy head held by the first of the hand or a sulky face buried into the palms can be giveaways of a gloomy mood, depression or sadness. People who understand the technique of hiding facial expressions know this. Thus, they always try to make sure that their head is held up high to better deceive you. When you are keen on them, there will be these occasions when they can no longer hold the head up and end up burying the face in their palms for some seconds before realizing that they may show you that they are lying. Careful analysis of the struggles not to support the head could reveal to you that they are faking their facial expression.

4. Struggling to relax the face

A relaxed face can easily build up a deceiving facial expression. For example, your son may have committed an offense in school and they come to report the matter to you, hoping to come out as victims. If your first glance on their faces shows them as being relaxed, you could actually be deceived and even get on the wrong side with the teachers. However, if you saw their faces were not relaxed even before they started the explanation, you can tell right away that there must be a problem somewhere. When you speak to someone and at one time their face is relaxed and at the other one it is not, that is a sign of a problem. Within a few minutes their face could be straight while at another it is steel and acting like a tough guy. This shows that they may have tried to relax it up to a certain point when they could do it no more. There is something here, take a deep look at their faces and you shall see it.

5. Silent lip movements

To be calm, some people speak to themselves. They may say something like "Calm down, you can do this. Just stay cool." If you are not careful, they may actually succeed in being calm and creating a falsified facial expression. Through a keen look at the lip movements, you may tell that the person has more things that they are hiding under their facial expressions.

Decoding Facial Expressions

The universality of facial expression has been subject to debate ever since Darwin's time to date. Some facial expressions seem to be universal while others are confined to particular zones. However, there are some expressions of the face which seem to be sending the same message among individuals from all corners of the world. This chapter decodes the hidden message in various facial expressions. This is an important factor because 80% of the emotions are shown and revealed on one's face. Do not just listen to the words, pay attention to what the face says.

#1: **Furrowed brow most often indicates to signs of discomfort**

The furrowed brow facial expression accurately represents what it means to feel and create negative emotions. When one starts to get stressed, anxious or angry, their brow is furrowed. Even if the individual may pretend to be all happy around you, this is a great giveaway!

#2: **Eye contact typically indicates interest and confidence**

Typically, when someone is telling the truth, they tend to look you directly in the eyes. This is called eye contact. Such individuals have immense confidence in whatever they are saying that they do not see the problem in facing you directly. When the speaker and the receiver maintain a direct and attentive eye contact, it could be translated that both parties are interested in the subject of discussion and that some level of truths are involved. One is also seen as being confident. The converse sends the message of shyness, lies or uninterested in all that's said.

#3: If the eyes are averted downwards, shame is probably involved

This is one of the most uniquely recognized facial expressions. In most cases, the eyes of the individuals are normally averted downward while the person wears a saddened and worried look. The head also takes a downward look, with a frowning or neutral mouth. In simpler terms, shame could be associated with submission. It's as if the individuals are sending the message that they have been caught when they least expected it and that they have no choice than to submit. For primates, when the dominant individual successfully forces the other side into submission, the losing side tend to look downward in submission.

In your observation of facial expressions, you will likely see shame in the other person's face. However, what you may not see is what cause that shame. The shame could be due to something they did and didn't like it or they were involved in some competition and lost. These will be manifested in broad ways thus some background information would guide you in coming up with a more effective conclusion.

#4: If they repeatedly touch the face, they are probably nervous

There are many things that can make someone nervous. When an individual is faced with a situation likely to cause one anxious, you will notice them repeatedly touching their face.

One may be having financial problems or thinking of changing jobs and all these emotions will build up in them to a point they can no longer take it. When that happens, they tend to bury their face in their hands and take in deep breathes.

These symptoms of anxiety or nervousness can grow to a larger extent that your normal life is interfered with.

#5: If you see their mouth and eyes are wide open simultaneously, they may be surprised

Gaping mouth and widened eyes are the trademarks for a surprised look. Surprise or shock as an emotion is closely associated with fear. The face made by a surprised person is one that instinctively forms. This occurs unconsciously to us and is triggered when something that we did not expect happens. When this unexpected event takes root, the eyes widen and the pupils expand so that they can cover more of the increased environment.

#6: Frowns and slanted eyebrows may display sad emotions being experienced

Unlike happiness, sadness assumes a less welcoming face. Many people find it easy to walk towards a happy person but will rarely have the same freedom when approaching a sad person. Sadness is facially expressed by a frown and slanted eyebrows. These are then coupled with feelings of loss and helplessness. Withdrawn individuals typically display this face. The expression originates in a simple manner: the features which show sadness are basically your usual facial features but in their reduced form. Everything tends to droop downward, but they seem not to be headed in any specific direction. It could as well be an indication of defeat, lack of initiative to engage others or giving up. Certain individuals couple the sadness facial expression with teary eyes (but this is not always a guarantee). One has to be careful when associating teary eyes with sadness because sometimes one could form tears as a result of too much joy.

#7: Clenched jaw or tightened neck shows stress

The two limbic responses are linked to the limbic system in the brain. The limbic system plays the crucial role of controlling how we react to threats, and display emotions.

When you notice someone missing the bus at stage, they will likely clench their jaws and rub their necks. Or the boss sends a letter to the staff that everyone will work over the weekend and all of a sudden the orbits of their eyes narrow as their chin lowers.

#8: Half-open eyelids and weak-looking shows tiredness

Half-open eyelids are the main facial expression that the person you are looking at is exhausted. In an attempt to stay awake, this person typically raises the eyebrows. When you perform too much of a task while allowing yourself no room for rest, fatigue soon kicks in. The face expresses this in a weak-like appearance, probably seeking sympathy from any onlookers. As fatigue takes over our bodies, the faces act as an indicator of the amount of energy we could be left with. It shows our level of functionality when we are in a team and the others can notice our capabilities.

#9: Infrequent blinking and eyes fixed on a particular thing shows they're probably focused

A focused facial expression tends to vary depending on the situation. If an individual is focused on a given task, they will have their eyes fixed on it. If the same individual is focused on a thought or idea, they tend to look upward with their eyes facing the side. You may also notice that they blink once in a very long time. An interesting part about how focus is facially expressed is when a person twists their tongue and will move it from side to side. Many are not aware that they are doing this. The phenomenon is referred to as motor dis-inhibition whereby a bigger percentage of your brain's energy is dedicated to the task while the remaining little energy keeps the body stagnant.

#10: Head scratching with the eyes gazing in the eye may indicate confusion

When one is confused, he/she is unaware of what direction to take. They have a couple of options to choose from, all of which seem viable. This is a state that can be expressed by the face. It is mostly characterized by the nose and forehead scrunched up and there may be an eyebrow which is higher than the other. The lips of the confused person are also pursed together while the actual confusion tends to be seen around the eyes. Confusion is an indicator that you lack some understanding and the expression itself comes about when the individual puts in more effort to properly understand the matter at hand.

Managing Personal Facial Expression

Knowing how to read facial expressions is as important as knowing how to manage the same. Managing your facial expression is a simple task that can have a significant impact on your life and communication skills. There are countless benefits that come with being able to manage your facial expression.

You may want to surprise someone but you do not want it to show or you may have decided to tell a story from a given perspective due to reasons best known to you and you do not want the other person to detect that. This chapter shows you how you can manage your facial expressions.

Increase your conscious alertness

Be more careful that you do not send out the wrong message from your unconscious 'neutral' mind through awkward facial displays. It is a common issue amongst human beings that they may not understand what to do with their faces. However, when you pay the right attention, you will be able to see beforehand what facial you have displayed and handle it in advance.

When you have a high conscious alertness, it means that you are able to change your interpretation of a situation immediately it takes place, therefore having an upper hand on the emotion and hence the resultant facial expression. Conscious alertness is able to penetrate the fast process that triggers a facial expression so that you can short-circuit the whole process. One way to increase your conscious alertness is to live in the NOW rather than the PAST. Being in the present implies that when something happens, your whole mind is available to perceive it.

Know your face

To control your facial expressions, you must understand your face. You can do this by resting your face and taking a picture of it. If you were the other person, would you initiate a small talk with someone sharing your resting face? You can also know your face by standing in front of the mirror. Keenly look at that face, and even try making mimics of various situations like sad, happy or surprised to know how you would look.

Take control of your face's muscles

Facial expressions are directed by the muscles in your face. When the brain sends a particular signal, it is these muscles that pick the signal and adjust accordingly. Thus, you need to manage these muscles if you are to feel that you are managing your facial expression. One of the ways to do this is by learning how to wiggle your ears. Stand in front of the mirror and practice. You may notice that you squint your eyes, raise the eyebrows or close and open the mouth several times. These are different facial muscles which you should learn to control. For example, when someone tells you something that is surprising but you do not come across as being surprised, try keep your eyes minimal because widely opened eyes will give you away.

Perform facial expressions while alone

Allow yourself some quality time in front of the mirror and exercise different facial expressions. Take note of the changes in your mood as you put on different facial expressions. Understand how the body would feel with a given facial look and how that changes when another look is worn. Synchronization of the body's emotions with your face is vital as it gives you an idea in advance of what a particular emotion would make your face look like. The only goal for you to do is manage the two to be in line when you want to pass across a particular message.

For example, as you speak with someone, make sure that you maintain eye contact with them at all times. Whether you are saying something that you believe in or not, maintaining eye contact is a show of confidence in oneself, hence confidence in your words.

Relax the mouth

Frown-shaped pout or neutral lips tend to be less inviting. Thus, make sure your facial muscles are relaxed by simply maintaining a small parting of your lips. When your facial muscles are relaxed, a warm message is sent by your face and this facial expression is easier to manage. Furthermore, a relaxed mouth turns up the corners of your mouth, making you look more appealing and approachable.

Visualize what you are talking about

In order to appear as though you mean what you are talking about, it is paramount that your facial expression matches your words. By visualizing what you are talking about, you essentially make pictures in your head that put some life into your words. As you speak, you connect to the image and focus on then translate that image into the appropriate facial expression. Facial expression that does not match the words being said delivers a mixed message.

Get feedback

Get someone you trust and ask them to make an evaluation of your face as you speak. This should be done in privacy. Are there any habits that you may have but are unaware of them? Is your facial expression expressive enough in association to what you speak?

How To Be a Pro at Reading Facial Expressions

Decoding people's facial expressions is one skill that you cannot afford to miss out. With such a skill, you get information about people which the average person wouldn't have. Very few individuals have this kind of skill. No wonder we have too many heartbreaks and broken deals. Remember that 80% of emotions are shown by the face. So, if you get to properly decode the facial expressions in advance, you will highlight behaviors that signal danger in the near future. This chapter takes you through the various ways in which you can become better at reading people's facial expressions.

#1: Differentiate between observing and looking

Most people look at others' faces, thinking they are observing them. Even though both observation and looking is done with the use of eyes, the two are completely different. They are mistakenly used to mean the other but that ought to change. Looking is when you see others without the intent of getting to know more than what is visible to the eye. You do not try to derive meaning out of the actions done by others nor do you try to commit anything to the brain. Observing has to do with seeing the actions performed by people and keeping the visions in mind so that you can make meaning out of them, posing questions. You perform deductions, that is, separating vital details from the unimportant ones, utilizing your careful observation to conclude.

Make sure that you know the two are different so that you do not waste time looking at people thinking you are observing them. In fact, in looking you will end up awkwardly staring at others and it may even earn you a smack in the face.

#2: Be curious

For you to decode one's facial expression, you must have some form of curiosity towards him/her. It is this curiosity that drives you to dedicate your time observing them. It is human nature to pay attention to what interests them. If you develop negative attitudes towards others, chances are you may not observe them diligently. That calls for an effort on your part to prevent your feelings or emotions from getting in the way of your observation. Even if you do not like somebody but you still have to observe them, make sure that you keep the dislike at bay or else you will achieve nothing.

Identify something that you find to be intriguing about others and curiously purpose to exploit it further. Understand that we all learn from each other and so even if they appear to be different, appreciate that and continue observing them. Is there somebody you do not like but they still have friends who are so fond of them? Curiosity would drive you into wanting to know why they have the following despite you despising them. If you spot some differences between you and others, curiosity would lead you into wanting to know why the differences exist.

#3: Say NO to judgment

Being judgmental is the number one thing that will block you from making effective observation of people. When you judge others, you feed your brain with the wrong information and block it from getting facts. For a good people observer, neutrality is prioritized. Observations are free of personal feelings since such elements are biased. When you involve prejudices, preconceived notions and personal feelings, you are not able to see what is there. You only get to see what you want to see. A good people observer knows how to ignore their personal feelings so that they can feed their brains with the right details for analysis.

To avoid being judgmental as you go about observing others, begin by taking a step back. Refrain from trying to enter into the other person's life and let them just be themselves. Do not try to make conclusions about whatever they do. Rather than thinking of a negative experience you had with them or saw them perform, see them for who they are – a person. If they drive a certain car, do not look at them in a certain way just because you associate the car with a particular social class. When you are neutral, you are able to see people clearly. The person driving a 'cheap car' may be building a multi-billion house just across the street. Your neighbor with an expensive car might have to work three jobs to pay for it.

#4: Stare more where possible

There is something about staring at people that makes you get finer details that had been previously concealed from your eyes. One of the ways to observe people is to stare at them and the things they like doing, but you must make sure you are not within the framework that might define you as being 'creepy.' We tend to encode more information from what the eyes sees as opposed to what is spoken or written. Stare as much as necessary for the eyes to pick relevant data and send it to the brain for analysis.

Staring at people can be a tricky engagement. Even from your own perspective, if you see somebody just staring at you, you will feel kind of awkward or may even want to react violently. Thus, your staring should be a purposeful stare but one that is concealed. If you can get your hands to videos involving such people and uploaded online, the better. You could lock yourself in a room and stare at the people in videos until you get what you are looking for. While in public, control the urge to stare to levels that let you get basic information.

#5: Avoid distractions

The reason as to why you may not perform a good observation is because you are distracted. As you go about your observation, a WhatsApp notification on your smartphone could force you to lose focus on what you were doing. The distractions are all over us, whether it's your to-do list, music or cell phones. The best way to focus on people's observation is to eliminate these distractions.

Remove your headphones as you interact with other people. Allow yourself to hear the surrounding sounds and probably what others are saying (but do not appear to be eavesdropping). If you are watching a video that has the person whom you are observing, concentrate on it as you listen to any conversations held. Rather than watching mindlessly, pay attention. Think about what they wore and why they acted in a particular way.

Don't Forget Your Free Gift!

***

As a way of saying thank you for your purchase, I'd like to give you a **Free** gift!

The Cruelest Face of "Love" Revealed' is your essential quick-start guide to help you detect & escape high-conflict personalities in your life.

»CLICK HERE to download your FREE Guide now!«

*** *The offer expires in 24 hours so go ahead click the link and grab your copy now!*

Discover how manipulative people use **fear**, **obligation**, and **guilt** to push your buttons and leave you completely numb!

Understand how they hook you so insidiously and deceptively, so you can stop feeling guilty about missing red flags.

» **Click Here to Get Your 100% Free Bonus Now!«**

The end ... almost!

If you enjoyed this book and found some benefit in reading this, I'd really like to hear from you.

Reader reviews are the lifeblood of any author's career.

I would be incredibly thankful if you could take just 60 seconds to write a brief review on Amazon, even if it's just a few sentences!

» Click here to leave a brief review on Amazon.«

Thank you for taking the time to share your thoughts!

References

Arabi, S. (2018) 3 powerful ways to heal from the toxic triangulation of narcissists. Retrieved from https://thoughtcat-alog.com/shahida-arabi/2017/05/3-powerful-ways-to-heal-from-the-toxic-triangulation-of-narcissists/

D., J. (2017) 20 most common manipulation techniques used by predators. Retrieved from https://www.learning-mind.com/manipulation-techniques/

Exploring Your Mind. Psychological manipulation techniques you may be a victim of. Retrieved from https://exploringyourmind.com/psychological-manipulation-techniques-you-may-be-a-victim-of/

Fon, R. (2017) 4 sure signs someone is trying to use psycholog-ical manipulation against you. Retrieved from https://iheartin-telligence.com/signs-psychological-manipulation/

Hall, K. (2012) Understanding Validation. Retrieved from https://blogs.psychcentral.com/emotionally-sensitive /2012/02/reasons-you-and-others-invalidate-your-emotional-experience/

Hill, T. (2017) 10 unbelievable behaviors of the narcis-sist. Retrieved from https://blogs.psychcentral.com/care-givers/2017/03/10-unbelievable-behaviors-of-the-narcissist/

Lancer, D. (2017) How to know if you're a victim of gaslight-ing. Retrieved from

https://www.psychologytoday.com/blog/toxic-relationships/

201801/how-know-if-youre-victim-gaslighting

Lancer, D. (2019) Covert tactics manipulators use to control and confuse you. Retrieved from https://www.psychologyto-day.com/intl/blog/toxic-relationships/201907/covert-tactics-manipulators-use-control-and-confuse-you

Luna, A. You're not going crazy. Retrieved from https://lon-erwolf.com/gaslighting/

Long, J. The power of validations: 5 things not to say UP-DATED. Retrieved from https://drjamielong.com/validation-5-things-not-to-say/

Murphy, B. (2015) 11 psychological tricks to manipulate people, ranked in order of pure evilness. Retrieved from https://www.inc.com/bill-murphy-jr/evil-psychological-tricks-to-manipulate-people.html

Ni, P. (2015) 14 signs of psychological and emotional manip-ulation. Retrieved from
https://www.psychologytoday.com/gb/blog/
communication-success/201510/14-signs-
psychological-and-emotional-manipulation

Ni, P. (2014) How to spot and stop manipulators. Retrieved from https://www.psychologytoday.com/intl/blog/
communication-success/201406/how-spot-
and-stop-manipulators

Passionate Learner (2019) 17 of a signs of a manipula-tor – never get deceived again. Retrieved from https://-pairedlife.com/problems/Spot-the-manipulator-in-your-life

POP (2019) 8 signs you have a manipulative partner. Re-trieved from https://www.powerofpositivity.com/manipulative-partner-signs/

POP (2019) Phrases manipulators use and how to respond. Retrieved from https://www.powerofpositivity.com/phrases-manipulators-use-how-respond/

POP (2019) 7 signs someone is trying to psychologically manipulate you. Retrieved from https://www.powerofpositivity.com/7-signs-someone-trying-psychologically-manipulate/

Sarkis, S. A. (2017) 11 Warning signs of gaslighting. Retrieved from

https://www.psychologytoday.com/blog/here-there-and-everywhere/201701/11-warning-signs-gaslighting

Wilkinson, A. (2017) What is Gaslighting? Retrieved from ttps://www.vox.com/culture/2017/1/21/14315372/what-is-gaslighting-gaslight-movie-ingrid-bergman